DOUGHNUTS: THE HOLE STORY

THE DISH ON THE DISH: A HISTORY OF YOUR FAVORITE FOODS

JULIE KNUTSON

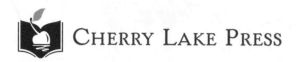

CHERRY LAKE PRESS

Published in the United States of America by Cherry Lake Publishing Group
Ann Arbor, Michigan
www.cherrylakepublishing.com

Reading Adviser: Reading Adviser: Beth Walker Gambro, MS, Ed., Reading Consultant, Yorkville, IL
Photo Credits: © SeventyFour/Shutterstock.com, cover, 1; © VasiliyBudarin/Shutterstock.com, 5;
   © Brent Hofacker/Shutterstock.com, 6, 9, 10; © BongkarnGraphic/Shutterstock.com, 8; © Courtesy
   of the Library of Congress, LC-DIG-anrc-17436, 13; © Courtesy of the Library of Congress,
   LC-DIG-anrc-17894, 14; © Courtesy of the Library of Congress, LC-USZC4-7915, 15; © / Courtesy
   of the Library of Congress, LC-DIG-hec-29856, 16; © James R. Martin/Shutterstock.com, 18;
   © YesPhotographers/Shutterstock.com, 21; © Bartosz Luczak/Shutterstock.com, 23;
   © Raimunda-losantos/Shutterstock.com, 24; © rittikorn poonwong/Shutterstock.com, 27;
   © beats1/Shutterstock.com, 28

Cherry Lake Press is an imprint of Cherry Lake Publishing Group.

Library of Congress Cataloging-in-Publication Data

Names: Knutson, Julie, author.
Title: Doughnuts : the hole story / by Julie Knutson.
Description: Ann Arbor, Michigan : Cherry Lake Publishing, [2022] | Series: The dish on the dish: a history
   of your favorite foods | Includes index. | Audience: Grades 4-6
Identifiers: LCCN 2021006134 (print) | LCCN 2021006135 (ebook) | ISBN 9781534187337 (hardcover) |
   ISBN 9781534188730 (paperback) | ISBN 9781534190139 (pdf) | ISBN 9781534191532 (ebook)
Subjects: LCSH: Doughnuts—History—Juvenile literature.
Classification: LCC TX770.D67 K55 2021 (print) | LCC TX770.D67 (ebook) | DDC 641.86/53—dc23
LC record available at https://lccn.loc.gov/2021006134
LC ebook record available at https://lccn.loc.gov/2021006135

Cherry Lake Publishing Group would like to acknowledge the work of the Partnership for 21st Century
Learning, a Network of Battelle for Kids. Please visit http://www.battelleforkids.org/networks/p21
for more information.

Printed in the United States of America
Corporate Graphics

ABOUT THE AUTHOR

About the author: Julie Knutson is an author who lives in northern Illinois with her
husband, son, and border collie. She prefers her pancakes with Nutella and bananas,
her pizza "Detroit-style," and her mac 'n' cheese with little green peas.

TABLE OF CONTENTS

First Plating

Around the world, they go by many names. There are powdered-sugar dusted **beignets** in New Orleans and buttery balushahi in Northern India. In Spain, there's the warming treat called *churros con chocolate*. In Canada, the United States, and France, there are beautifully braided **crullers**, glazed to perfection.

Whether deep-fried or oven-baked, they're a beloved global sensation. They're DOUGHNUTS, the treat of which animated character Homer Simpson once wondered, "Is there anything they can't do?"

But when and where does the story of these humble rings of dough begin?

Homer Simpson's doughnut has pink glaze and rainbow sprinkles.

Pączkis fillings come in many flavors. Popular flavors are lemon and raspberry.

Believe it or not, humans have enjoyed sweetened fried dough for thousands of years. Residents of the Roman Empire fried dough and coated it with honey. Across the ancient Middle East, recipes have been recorded for zalabia—puffy fritters drenched in sugar syrup and rose water—from the 10th century! In China, people have been eating youtiao since at least the Middle Ages.

[21ST CENTURY SKILLS LIBRARY]

The doughnut as Americans know it likely came from the Netherlands in the early colonial period. Dutch immigrants supposedly brought olykoeks, literally "oily cakes," to New Amsterdam. These early doughnuts consisted of masses of dough fried in oil. That explains the dough . . . but what about the "nut"?

A Holiday Treat

In many religious traditions, doughnuts are a special holiday treat. During the celebration of Hanukkah, jelly-filled doughnuts called sufganiyot are deep-fried in oil. The cooking oil represents the oil said to have miraculously burned for 8 days at the temple in Jerusalem, the basis for this holiday.

Doughnuts make their way into Christian celebrations too. The season of Lent marks the 46 days before Easter. The day before Lent begins, sometimes called "Fat Tuesday" or "Shrove Tuesday," is a day for enjoying all the food and drink that's off-limits during the **fasting** of Lent. In Poland, people splurge on pączkis with custard or jelly centers. In some Pennsylvania Dutch communities, **fastnachts** are prepared. As legend holds, making these doughnuts was a way of emptying the pantry of tempting treats like sugar and butter before the Lenten fast.

Nuts are a great addition to a sweet treat.

According to one story, a 19th-century New England woman named Elizabeth Gregory added a filling of hazelnuts and walnuts to her dough mix. The dough was also spiced with nutmeg and lemon rind. Gregory's creations literally paired "dough" with "nuts." The ingredients of this fried, hand-held food provided nutrition for sailors during long sea voyages, on which **scurvy** was a common sickness.

[21ST CENTURY SKILLS LIBRARY]

Glazed doughnuts are the most popular type of doughnut in the United States.

A doughnut hole makes the perfect bite-sized treat.

Elizabeth's son, sea captain Hanson Gregory, is often credited for giving the doughnut its hole. But just how and why did this happen? There are a few versions of the story. In one, Captain Gregory was steering his ship during a storm. Helming the wheel required his full concentration. So, he skewered the doughnut on one of the wheel's spokes until he could again focus on eating. In another, Hanson was bothered by the doughy cake's raw center. This led him to use the lid of a tin to poke out a hole. On return to land, he suggested frying them as rings so they cooked evenly. In yet another? Well, he just didn't like the nuts at the center of the ring, so he poked them out.

At age 85, Hanson Gregory recalled the birth of the doughnut's hole. Here's the version that he settled on in his elder years: "Now in them [sic] days . . . they was [sic] just 'fried cakes' and 'twisters.' . . . They used to fry all right around the edges, but when you had the edges done the insides was [sic] all raw dough. . . . Well, I says [sic] to myself, 'Why wouldn't a space inside solve the difficulty?' I thought at first I'd take one of the strips and roll it around, then I got an inspiration . . . I took the cover off the ship's tin pepper box, and—I cut into the middle of that doughnut the first hole ever seen by mortal eyes!"

CHAPTER 2

Migrations

During the 20th century, the doughnut got elevated to superstar status. In the popular imagination, it helped people endure hardships ranging from the horrors of World War I to the economic struggles of the **Great Depression**. A wonder of industrial food production, it drew admirers at the 1934 World's Fair in Chicago, Illinois. As chains like Krispy Kreme® and Dunkin' Donuts® expanded in the 1950s, doughnuts ruled the pastry world.

The doughnut's makeover as "heroic food" started in World War I. American soldiers fighting in Europe were nicknamed "doughboys." While this term dates from the Civil War, it gained

Soldiers lined up for coffee and doughnuts each morning.

Women made doughnuts in the basement of the American Red Cross Headquarters in Paris, France, in 1918.

popularity because of efforts to cheer up soldiers fighting on the front line. As a way to boost **morale**, women volunteers with the Salvation Army called "Doughnut Lassies" distributed doughnuts in the trenches. According to a Salvation Army online history:

> *"The pastries were virtually unknown in the States at the time and proved so popular that when the American soldiers returned home, their demand for the sweet treat created the culinary phenomenon of the doughnut."*

(Quoted by Deke Farrow, *The Sacramento Bee*, June 4, 2016.)

Posters like this were common during World War I.

Street vendors selling treats and doughnuts began
popping up around cities after World War I.

The doughnut's boom after World War I was sparked by the fondness of returning soldiers for the treat, plus a key technological development. In 1920, New York baker Adolph Levitt **automated** doughnut production to keep up with demand. By 1931, his doughnuts were being sold **wholesale** to bakeries all over the country. Levitt, a Russian refugee, soon had a doughnut-making empire worth an estimated $25 million!

In the 1930s, the doughnut's popularity showed no signs of slowing down. Doughnuts were even featured in movies. Levitt's automation process was celebrated at the 1934 World's Fair in Chicago, Illinois. They were praised as a "food of progress." As a 5-cent treat during the Great Depression, most people could afford them. During the hard times of the 1930s, some doughnut shops

A 1919 essay contest entry written by a young boy suggests just how much support the Doughboys enjoyed. The boy wrote, "To think that a little ring of dough twined around a small piece of atmosphere could be made to cheer the heart and steady the nerve is wonderful, and yet that's what the Doughnut did for the Doughboy." —published in the Fort Scott Daily Tribune & Fort Scott Daily Monitor, *Fort Scott, Kansas, April 30, 1919.*

The "Hot Doughnuts Now" neon sign at Krispy Kreme® lets customers know when fresh doughnuts are being made.

even included encouraging messages with their products. One said, "As you go through life make this your goal: Watch the doughnut, not the hole."

As America entered World War II in 1941, the doughnut again played a morale-boosting role. This time, Red Cross volunteers nicknamed "Doughnut Dollies" served on the war's European front. The standards to join this program were high. Applicants had to be college-educated, at least 25 years old, and have excellent references. Only one in six women who applied were accepted. In England and elsewhere in Europe, they served up massive numbers of doughnuts to American soldiers. Historian Carolyn Apple reports that in December 1944 alone, "205 Red Cross women in Great Britain served 4,659,728 doughnuts to the troops."

After the war, the United States experienced a period of economic prosperity marked by the rise of the **suburbs**. **Franchise** businesses sprung up across the country, meeting a new appetite for fast, standardized food. Chains like Krispy Kreme®, which had been around since the 1930s, rapidly expanded across the South. Newer chains like Dunkin' Donuts® established a foothold in the Northeast. Within 10 years of opening, Dunkin' Donuts® had 100 retail locations across the country. Today, there are more than 12,000 locations worldwide, with stores in 45 countries. And as we'll see next, recipes and mixes continue to change to meet the demands of new generations.

The doughnut as a health food? Today, that might seem like a bit of a stretch. But in 1934, Roe Wells, vice president of the Doughnut Corporation of America, presented a different view. Wells told a reporter, "Our doughnut is considered by the highest medical authorities as being beneficial to children as well as adults." —published in the Miami Herald, *October 19, 1934.*

CHAPTER 3

Evolution and Wild Variations

In the United States alone, more than 10 billion doughnuts are produced each year. Canada adds another 1 billion to that total. You can choose a traditional glazed doughnut or try a fancy new flavor, like hibiscus or red velvet. There are **cronuts**, donarts, and donnolis to tempt your tastebuds. But doughnuts have always been far more than a North American food sensation. Let's spin the globe to see what you might enjoy in different corners of the world.

We start our journey in Kyoto, Japan. Rise, shine, and head to the Nishiki Market for a tofu doughnut! You can add honey, chocolate, or caramel. And save room for soy-based ice cream before heading to our next destination!

Doughnuts can be filled with any flavor, like plum or black licorice.

In Delhi, India, savor a balushahi, a nearly bite-sized doughnut made with yogurt and cooked in **ghee**. Balushahi are glazed and can be garnished with pistachios, saffron, or rose petals.

Next up? Rwanda for mandazi. These small doughnuts amp up the flavor with coconut milk, cardamom, and cinnamon. They're often triangular but can also be circular. You can top them with cinnamon or sugar.

On any day of the year in Madrid, Spain, you can enjoy *churros con chocolate* at the Chocolatería San Ginés. This café has been operating since 1894 and offers deep-fried churros that are best dipped in thick drinking chocolate.

Haven't quite had your share of fried dough? Try pumpkin puree-infused **sopaipillas** in Chile. These fried circles of dough can be eaten for breakfast, lunch, dinner, dessert, or as a snack. Top with powdered sugar or drizzle with honey or jam for a tasty treat.

In 2012, KFC® restaurants in Singapore debuted a new menu item, fish doughnuts. Yes, it's exactly what it sounds like: fish molded into a ring and deep-fried into a doughnut shape. This item was available alongside shrimp stars and more traditional KFC® fare. What do you think? Would you try it?

Churros have been around since the 16th century.
They are coated in cinnamon sugar.

Cronuts combine the flaky layers of croissants with doughnuts.

It all comes full circle in New Orleans, Louisiana, with a beignet, a tasty treat with French roots. These fluffy pillows of **choux** flour topped with powdered sugar are best enjoyed with friends, as they are typically served up three at a time. Plus, it helps to have a friend around to point out the spots where all that stray powdered sugar has landed!

Cronuts

What do you get when you cross a croissant with a doughnut? A cronut! In 2013, this hybrid food appeared at New York's Dominique Ansel Bakery. It was an immediate sensation. Long lines of curious customers soon lined up to taste test the new invention. *Time* magazine even called it one of the year's 25 best inventions.

The cronut craze quickly spread to other cities across the world. Soon, foodies in San Francisco, California, and Houston, Texas, were lining up to sample cronuts of their own. Other food mash-ups also followed. They included the cragel (croissant-bagel), the donart (doughnut-tart), and the donnoli (doughnut-cannoli).

CHAPTER 4

Make Your Own!

You don't have to travel around the world to enjoy doughnuts! Believe it or not, with the help of an adult, you can make doughnuts at home. Here's a super-easy recipe to get you started.

INGREDIENTS:

- 1 package of biscuit dough
- Vegetable oil
- Outer coating of your choice, such as cinnamon sugar, powdered sugar, frosting, or sprinkles

DIRECTIONS:

1. Open the biscuit package. Make a hole in the center of each biscuit. Looks like a doughnut, right?
2. Have an adult pour a generous amount of oil into a frying pan or wok. Heat the oil.

Be careful when working with hot oil.

3. Have an adult add the dough rings to the hot oil. Let the doughnuts cook for 30 seconds on each side, then flip them with a slotted spoon. After 1 to 2 minutes, they should be fully cooked!

4. Transfer the doughnuts to a paper towel to cool.

5. Once cooled, add coatings. If you want a sugar crust, pour the sugar into a plastic bag, add the doughnuts, and shake. If you opt for frosting, use a butter knife to spread across the surface.

Doughnuts can come with all sorts of toppings. The possibilities are endless!

10 wHOLEly Fascinating Facts

- **Per capita**, Canada boasts more doughnut shops than any other nation. In terms of actual doughnut consumption, Canadians also take the cake.

- In May 2020, Leah Shutkever of Birmingham, England, broke the record for most jam doughnuts eaten in 3 minutes. Shutkever ate 10 doughnuts in that time!

- Can you make art with doughnuts? You bet! The record for the world's largest doughnut mosaic was set in Luiv, Ukraine, on January 7, 2012. Made for a Christmas festival, this edible work of art featured 7,040 sugary treats.

- Imagine a skyscraper of doughnuts! Credit for the tallest doughnut structure goes to the Jewish Life Center in Johannesburg, South Africa. As part of 2018's Hanukkah festivities, a tiered tower measuring 59.8 inches (152 centimeters) was built.

- The record for the largest filled doughnut has gone unbroken for nearly 30 years! In 1993, two bakeries in Utica, New York, worked with the local radio station to produce a 3,739-pound (1,696 kilogram) creation.

- The Canadian doughnut chain Tim Hortons accounts for nearly 25 percent of all fast-food sales in the country.

- In 2017, the Manila Social Club in Miami, Florida, unveiled a doughnut that cost $1,200! "The Golden Cristal Ube" was sprinkled with gold leaf and filled with champagne.

- The largest doughnut bakery in the United States is Entenmann's Bakery in Carlisle, Pennsylvania.

- According to the Food Network, "More than 55 million doughnuts would be needed to reach across the United States from Long Beach, California, to Long Island, New York."

- This fact also is courtesy of the Food Network: "It would take 3,660 doughnuts to reach the top of the Statue of Liberty."

Timeline

1847 Sea captain Hanson Gregory allegedly puts the first hole in the doughnut.

1918 The doughnut and "Doughnut Lassies" are praised for boosting the morale of troops during World War I.

1920 New York baker Adolph Levitt invents a machine that automates doughnut production.

1934 The doughnut is labeled the "food of progress" at the Chicago World's Fair in Illinois.

1937 The first Krispy Kreme® store opens in Winston-Salem, North Carolina.

1938 National Doughnut Day is established as a holiday, partly to honor the "Doughnut Lassies" who served during World War I.

1948 Open Kettle opens in Quincy, Massachusetts. It changes its name to Dunkin' Donuts® in 1950.

1964 Popular Canadian chain Tim Hortons is founded.

1997 The Smithsonian Institution's National Museum of American History exhibits the "Ring King" doughnut maker from Krispy Kreme®. It celebrates the doughnut's place in American food culture.

2012 KFC® begins selling fish doughnuts at branches in Singapore.

2013 The cronut is first sold in New York City, New York.

Further Reading

BOOKS

Higgins, Nadia. *Fun Food Inventions*. Minneapolis, MN: Learner Publishing, 2014.

Miles, David. *Donuts: The Hole Story*. Sanger, CA: Familius, 2018.

Miller, Pat, and Vincent X. Kirsch (illus.). *The Hole Story of the Doughnut*. New York, NY: Houghton Mifflin Harcourt, 2016.

WEBSITES

DHCA—World War II: Donut Dollies & the American Red Cross
www.history.delaware.gov/ww-ii-donut-dollies-the-american-red-cross
Check out this webpage for a historical look at Donut Dollies.

Smithsonian—Doughnut vs. Donut
www.si.edu/spotlight/doughnut
Check out this webpage to learn more about doughnuts in American history.

Smithsonian Magazine—The History of the Doughnut
www.smithsonianmag.com/history/the-history-of-the-doughnut-150405177
Check out this website for more history on the doughnut.

MYSTERYdoug—Why Do We Call Them Doughnuts?
www.mysterydoug.com/mysteries/dough-nuts
Watch this video to learn how doughnuts got their name.

GLOSSARY

automated (AW-tuh-may-tuhd) the use of machines to do work previously done by people

beignets (BAYN-yays) powdered-sugar doughnuts made famous in New Orleans

choux (SHOO) a pastry dough made of butter, water, flour, and eggs

cronuts (KROH-nuhtz) pastries crossed between a croissant and a doughnut

crullers (KRUH-luhrs) twisted deep-fried pastries

fastnachts (FAHSH-nahkts) Pennsylvania Dutch doughnuts traditionally eaten on Fat Tuesday

fasting (FAST-ing) not eating for a period of time or avoiding eating some foods

franchise (FRAN-chize) a company's license to an individual to own and operate one of their businesses

ghee (GEE) a clarified butter often used in India

Great Depression (GRAYT di-PRESH-uhn) the period of global economic decline that lasted from 1929 until 1939

morale (muh-RAHL) the state of mind or mental condition of a person or group

per capita (PUHR KAH-puh-tuh) the number for each person

scurvy (SKUR-vee) a disease caused by a lack of vitamin C

sopaipillas (soh-pye-PEE-uhs) deep-fried pastries common in Mexico and South America

suburbs (SUHB-urbs) small communities near large cities

wholesale (HOHL-sayl) when one company sell goods in bulk to another business, which resells them

INDEX